SPORTS GREAT
LARRY
BIRD

—Sports Great Books—

Sports Great Charles Barkley (ISBN 0-89490-386-1)

Sports Great Larry Bird (ISBN 0-89490-368-3)

Sports Great Roger Clemens (ISBN 0-89490-284-9)

Sports Great John Elway (ISBN 0-89490-282-2)

Sports Great Patrick Ewing (ISBN 0-89490-369-1)

Sports Great Bo Jackson (ISBN 0-89490-281-4)

Sports Great Magic Johnson (Revised and Expanded) (ISBN 0-89490-348-9)

Sports Great Michael Jordan (ISBN 0-89490-370-5)

Sports Great Joe Montana (ISBN 0-89490-371-3)

Sports Great Hakeem Olajuwon (ISBN 0-89490-372-1)

Sports Great David Robinson (ISBN 0-89490-373-X)

Sports Great Darryl Strawberry (ISBN 0-89490-291-1)

Sports Great Isiah Thomas (ISBN 0-89490-374-8)

Sports Great Herschel Walker (ISBN 0-89490-207-5)

SPORTS GREAT
LARRY
BIRD

Jack Kavanagh

—Sports Great Books—

ENSLOW PUBLISHERS, INC.

Bloy St. & Ramsey Ave.   P.O. Box 38
Box 777   Aldershot
Hillside, N.J. 07205   Hants GU12 6BP
U.S.A.   U.K.

Library of Congress Cataloging-in-Publication Data

Kavanagh, Jack
    Sports great Larry Bird / Jack Kavanagh.
        p. cm. — (Sports great books)
    Includes index.
    Summary: Describes the life and career of the noted Boston Celtics basketball
player, from his childhood to the present.
    ISBN 0-89490-368-3
    1. Bird, Larry, 1956– —Juvenile literature. 2. Basketball players—United
States—Biography—Juvenile literature. 3. Boston Celtics (Basketball
team)—Juvenile literature. [1. Bird, Larry, 1956– . 2. Basketball players.] I. Title.
II. Series.
GV884.B57B38 1992
796.323'092—dc20
[B]
                                      91-41525
                                          CIP
                                          AC

Printed in the United States of America

10 9 8 7 6 5 4 3 2 1

Photo Credits: Bob Breidenbach

Cover Photo: Bob Breidenbach

Contents

Chapter 1

Larry Bird had never heard the fans shout, "We're Number One!" Not in high school, not in college, and, so far, not as a Celtic. Larry had never played on a state or national championship team. He had been a star player in high school and college. His teams had been eliminated in the final round in two championship tournaments—first in high school and next in college. In his second season as a professional player, Larry Bird got another chance to play for a championship.

The 1980–81 season ended with the Boston Celtics tied with last year's NBA champions. The Philadelphia 76ers and the Boston Celtics had each won sixty-two games and lost twenty. Now they had to battle it out in the Eastern Conference playoffs. Whichever team won would meet the Western Conference playoff winner. That series would decide the National Basketball Association championship.

When Philadelphia won three of the first four games, it looked bad for Bird and the Celtics. One more Sixers' win and it was all over. Philadelphia even led, 109–103, in the fifth game with just 90 seconds to play. But the Celtics snatched

Larry Bird, called by some the greatest all-around basketball player of all time.

the victory by running off eight points while holding the Sixers scoreless.

Even so, it still seemed to be a lost cause for Boston. The next game would be played in Philadelphia, and the Celtics had lost their last eleven games at the Spectrum. The noisy Sixers fans made it tough on visiting teams. Yet, even though the Celtics fell behind by 17 points, they caught up with two seconds left to play. Cedric Maxwell put in two free throws for a 100–98 Celtics' win. The series was tied, and the teams would go back to Boston to settle matters.

However, it was the Sixers who led all the way until late in the final quarter of the deciding game. They were ahead by six points when Larry Bird took over. He stole a pass from the great Sixers forward Julius Erving. Larry whipped the ball to Tiny Archibald, who was fouled. Tiny sank both free throws. Next Larry picked off another Sixer pass. He fed it to Robert Parish, who tossed in a turnaround jumper. Then Larry Bird was fouled by Julius Erving and calmly swished two free throws through the nets. The score was tied at 89–89.

With only seconds to play, Erving drove for a layup, but Larry leaped high and swatted the ball away. When another Sixer, Darryl Dawkins, swooped in for another layup, he missed, and Larry came down with the rebound. He took off along the left sideline, dribbling toward the basket. Then he stopped, took aim, and banked in the tiebreaker for a Celtics' lead, 91–89. The game ended seconds later with Boston a one-point winner, 91–90.

Larry Bird told the reporters who crowded into the Celtics' dressing room, "I wanted to take the last shot." When the game is on the line, Larry Bird always wants the job of winning it.

With the dangerous Sixers eliminated, the NBA final round was expected to be easy for the Celtics. The winner of the Western Conference was Houston. Boston had beaten the Rockets the last thirteen times the two teams met. However, the Celtics were in for a letdown after their furious battles with the Sixers. They opened in the Boston Garden, but Houston led all the way. Finally, Larry Bird made what the Celtics' general manager Red Auerbach, of the 1960 and 1970s, called "the greatest play I have ever seen." After his 18-foot shot bounced off the rim, Larry raced in for the rebound. As he flew through the air, he shifted the ball to his left hand. Just before he crashed among the photographers along the baseline, he flipped the ball toward the basket, and it went in. The Boston fans were on their feet. The hard-charging Celtics ran off eight points, and Larry sank a final lay-up with 19 seconds to go. That gave Boston a 98–95 win in the opening game.

The NBA championship series was not over yet. Houston won two of the next three games. Larry Bird was in a rare shooting slump. He did what he always does when this happens. He made up for it with other parts of his game. He led both teams in assists and steals and battled Moses Malone, Houston's star, to a draw in rebounds. Even without Bird's usual point totals, the team play of the Celtics brought them a 109–80 win in the fifth game. They needed one more victory to become champions, and Larry's slump ended in game six. He scored 27 points, getting the critical ones in the final minutes. The Houston Rockets did not give up easily. Three times in the last minutes they came within three points of the lead. Each time the Rockets got close, Larry Bird stopped them. He hit on a 15-foot jumper. Then he lobbed a pass to Cedric Maxwell for a three-pointer from beyond the 26-foot circle. Finally he added his own three-pointer to put the game on ice. Boston won, 102–91. The Celtics were NBA champs for the fourteenth time, but for Larry Bird it was his first ever.

The Celtics defeated the Houston Rockets for Larry Bird's first championship.

Larry Bird, the greatest all-around player in basketball history according to many experts, had not been a "one man gang." Just the opposite was true. He has always been a dedicated team player. The NBA title was a team championship. His accurate passes to teammates led to points being scored. They counted just as much as those he personally put in the basket. Of all the statistics, "assists" is by far the most important to Larry Bird.

Over the years, Red Auerbach had become known for his huge "victory cigar" after Boston Celtics' triumphs. When a critical game was won, he would "light up." The happy Larry Bird snatched Red's cigar and took a few puffs himself. He had plenty to celebrate.

When the Celtics arrived back in Boston, they were paraded through the city's crowded streets. Larry waved to more people than he had ever seen before in his life. They cheered him and his Celtics teammates. Larry Bird now played on the best basketball team in the world. Back in Indiana, it had been Larry's fate to be the best player on a team from a small-town high school. In college he had dropped out of Indiana University, a national powerhouse, and gone to the much smaller Indiana State. Even when he joined the Boston Celtics, a team that had won more championships than any other professional basketball team, they had become losers. The year before Larry Bird joined them the Celtics won only 29 games and lost 53. The next season, with Bird taking charge, they won 61 and lost only 21. They improved by an incredible 32 games. They lost in the Eastern Conference Finals to Philadelphia 4–1 that first year.

Then for the 1980–81 season the Celtics added two key players. Robert Parish, 7 feet, and Kevin McHale, 6 feet, 10 inches, were able to control the ball under the baskets. Along with Cedric Maxwell, Tiny Archibald, M. L. Carr and Chris

Ford, Coach Bill Fitch was able to put together a team for Larry Bird to lead to victory.

In the Boston Garden, where the Celtics play their home games, championship banners are hung from the rafters. Each shows a year when the Boston Celtics won the NBA championship. There are 16 banners hanging high above the floor. The first was won in 1957, when the NBA had just eight teams. There were only four teams in each division. Today there are 27 teams and four divisions. In the early years there were fewer teams to beat, and the playoffs were much shorter. The Celtics won the championship eight years straight, from 1959 to 1966. That was the time when the immortal Bill

Boston Celtics fans crowd the city's streets when their team brings home a championship.

Russell was the dominant player in basketball. For many years he was considered the greatest player of all time. Red Auerbach, who had coached Russell, always insisted that Russell was the best player of all time. Finally, even Auerbach had to concede that, great as Russell had been, Larry Bird was the better all-around player. There are fewer championship banners hanging from the rafters of the Boston Garden from the Bird era than from the Russell era. Larry's Celtics have won three times so far. Russell's Celtics won eleven championships. But now the schedules are longer, and the teams are better balanced. The rules have been changed to reduce the "home court advantage," which used to favor the division winners.

What counted most with Larry Bird was that he was a member of a championship team at last. As the team's leader he could have told the people of Boston the victory was dedicated to them. Instead, he remembered how disappointed his friends and neighbors had been when tiny Springs Valley High School had failed to win the Indiana high school state championship in 1975. Larry Bird made a point of dedicating his share of the Celtics' victory to the folks back home. Then he said good-bye to Boston. He went home to where he still lives between basketball seasons, the rural community of French Lick, Indiana.

Chapter 2

If some babies are born to grow up to become basketball players, Larry Bird fits the description. He was born on Pearl Harbor Day, December 7, 1956. There were three older children, but none had come into the world the size of their baby brother, Larry Joe. He weighed 11 pounds, 12 ounces, and was 23 inches long. His parents were of Irish and Scottish descent, and there was Native American blood on both sides.

The blond-haired infant was doing push-ups when he was three months old and walked alone when he was nine months old. In his first year he had torn apart several cribs and a playpen. After that he shared a regular bed with his older brothers, Mike and Mark.

Georgia Kerns had married Joe Bird on September 20, 1951. She was twenty-one and the tallest of seven children. The large Kerns family was poor. Almost everyone in the region was. The Birds, who had an even bigger family, were even worse off than most of their neighbors. Larry's father, Joe Bird, had been a great athlete as a teenager but never even played high school sports. He enlisted in the United States

Bird uses his body to keep his opponent from getting near the ball after a tipoff.

Navy in 1944, when he was eighteen, and saw battle action in the Pacific. He was restless when the war ended, and in 1951 he joined the army for the Korean War. He was a combat infantryman and came home with terrible nightmares. These were to severely disturb him the rest of his life.

The Bird and Kerns families were typical of the people who lived in Orange County. It was the poorest county in southern Indiana. A lot of kids dropped out of school, and very few ever went to college. Many left the area to look for better-paying jobs. Those who stayed behind farmed, did odd jobs, or worked in small factories. At one time French Lick had been a famous health resort. Wealthy people came to use the natural hot springs. The water was bottled and shipped around the world. The resort industry employed many local people. During World War II, when travel restrictions prevented major league baseball teams from going south for spring training, the Chicago Cubs got ready for the 1944 and 1945 seasons in French Lick. Then the big resorts closed, and the local people lost their jobs. To make ends meet, Georgia Bird worked two jobs to bring in $100 a week. But it cost $125 to feed the family.

Joe Bird went from job to job, making good money as a furniture finisher, but his paycheck rarely came home with him on payday. He would spend his money in bars before he ever got home to his family.

Larry Bird grew up in a troubled family. His grandmother, Lizzie Kerns, though, was a gentle and caring woman who helped Georgia raise her many children. After Larry was born, two more boys joined the family. Larry was a particular favorite of his grandmother and lived at her house more than he did in his own home. The Birds moved often, unable to pay the rent. They would take their furniture to one ramshackle house after another. One thing that always went along was the basketball hoop that was nailed up behind the house. After Larry Bird became a professional basketball player, he built his mother a house. He filled it with new furniture. This time they did not move the old basketball hoop. Instead, Larry had a regulation basketball court built beside the new house.

There was a lot of love among the Birds. Christmas was always made special, even if money had to be borrowed to buy toys. The first gift Larry remembers getting was a basketball. He left it behind the wood-burning stove Christmas night, and in the morning it was covered with bumps and no longer round. It did not matter to Larry. He carried it with him everywhere.

Larry's older brothers, Mike and Mark, set the pace for Larry to become an athlete. They made their kid brother pitch batting practice and chase down basketballs. Larry grew up like other youngsters in the rough environment of French Lick and the nearby towns. Sports, hunting and fishing, and just hanging out were what kids did. Today, when Larry Bird locks the door of his expensive home in Boston at the end of the season, those are the things he does when goes back to Indiana for the summer.

Larry learned from his brothers that he had to keep up with his schoolwork so he could play on the athletic teams. Mark and Mike both played sports for the district high school. Mike was the best and went on to college. When Larry made the high school varsity team, he was given number 33. It had been his brother Mike's number. He has worn that number ever since. In college and in the NBA, Larry Bird is number 33. When he ends his career, the Boston Celtics will retire his uniform number. They already have back at Indiana State and Springs Valley High School.

Larry was good at all sports. He might have become a great quarterback. The way he passes a basketball the length of the court gives an idea how good he could have been. He always played games with older boys so he could test his developing skills. He played the outfield and shortstop in baseball. One year they made up a team just of the Bird brothers and their cousins, and Larry was the best player they had.

However, basketball was his first choice. From the start it consumed him. He played endlessly. He would ride his bike to any place there was a game. If there were not enough players for a regular game, they would use half the court and play three on a side. If that could not be done, he would shoot baskets with another boy. They would take turns chasing

Boston fans hold up Larry's number 33. Larry has worn that number ever since high school, when he took it over from his older brother Mike.

rebounds. If no one else showed up, Larry would take his shots and go after the ball himself. As long as there was a basket and a ball, Larry would practice. All through his career he has always been the first player in the gym and the last to leave it. Constant practice has always been Larry's trademark. It is the reason he improved his game season after season. His shooting average improved even after he became an All-Star.

Larry Bird developed slowly on the high school team. Even though he practiced endlessly, he was not a star at first. Then during his junior year, he became tall enough to dominate in high school competition. Over one summer he grew six inches. Suddenly he was 6 feet 9 inches, and the coach, Gary Holland, switched him to center.

Even so, in Indiana it is hard to get recognition when you play for a school in a small town. High school basketball is almost a religion in the state. Basketball was invented in western Massachusetts by Dr. James Naismith in the winter of 1891–92. He was a teacher at the YMCA college in Springfield. His graduates took the game with them when they went to work at YMCAs in other states. Indiana was the first state outside of Massachusetts to take up basketball. It was the perfect game for a state with many small farming towns. There was great rivalry, especially in sports, between the towns. Basketball was made to order for them. The season started right after the fall harvest and went on until spring planting. High school gyms held more people than lived in town.

Because Larry was injured as a sophomore, he did not really develop as a player until his junior year. As a senior, he led the whole state of Indiana in scoring. He averaged over 30 points a game. He scored 55 points in one game and pulled down 38 rebounds in another. Larry became a real leader. He got his teammates to the gym at 6:30 in the morning to practice shooting fouls. It almost paid off when Springs Valley just missed winning its regional tournament. However, the one boy who had always skipped early morning practice missed four free throws in a row at the end of the final game. The fans of the high school team were disappointed. However, they looked forward to Larry Bird's college career.

Chapter 3

Even before his team made the state finals, Larry Bird had been spotted by Bobby Knight, head coach at Indiana University. The folks of French Lick, Larry's hometown, were excited. The best players were at Indiana University. Larry was not sure he was ready to go to a big university. There were 30,000 students. He was only seventeen years old. He had never been out of the state except to play in a tournament. He was on the All-Star Indiana squad when they played the Kentucky boys at Louisville.

Larry Bird finally accepted the scholarship at Indiana University. He reached the campus in Bloomington for preseason practice, but in less than a month he went home. The coach, Bobby Knight, gave him no help. Larry roomed with another boy whose family had money. His clothes filled the closets in the room. Larry owned only a few extra pair of blue jeans, some T-shirts, and the suit he had worn to his high school graduation. Discouraged and lonely, the seventeen-year-old suddenly went home. Back in French Lick, many people were disappointed when Larry left college. When the greatest basketball player ever to come out of Springs Valley School took a job working on a garbage truck, they felt let down.

It was not until a year later that Larry Bird went back to college. This time he went to the much smaller Indiana State. He lost a year of eligibility to play intercollegiate basketball because he changed schools. By 1975 Larry Bird's life had changed in other ways. His parents had divorced, and then his father had died. Soon after he enrolled at Indiana State, Larry married a cheerleader. It did not last long. Yet, after the divorce, Larry learned he was the father of a daughter.

Basketball became even more important to Larry Bird. When he was not in class, he was in the gym. He practiced over and over, always improving his game. He could not play on the Indiana State team during the 1975–76 season. They had a 12–12 record. The next year the Sycamores lost only three games. Once Larry was eligible to play, they jumped to a 25–3 record in 1976–77. He averaged 33 points and 13 rebounds a game.

The next year Indiana State won 23 games while Larry averaged 30 points a game. He had one more year to play college basketball. However, because he had lost a year of eligibility when he dropped out of Indiana University, the NBA could draft him. When the Boston Celtics claimed him, Larry had a problem. He needed money. However, he had told his mother he would be the first in the family to graduate from college. Boston would have to wait. Larry played his final year at Indiana State.

What a year it was! Bird led all college players in scoring. Indiana State went through their schedule without losing a game. They won the Missouri Valley Conference title. They were Number One there, but it only gave them a place in the big National Collegiate Athletic Association postseason tournament. The NCAA is the real test for college teams. Indiana State rolled right along. They ran their winning streak to 33 games and reached the "Final Four."

Bird scored 35 points to edge out DePaul in a semifinal game, 76–74. Now came the big test. Larry Bird and Indiana State would meet Magic Johnson and Michigan State. Both players were 6 feet, 9 inches. Larry played forward, and Magic was a superstar at guard. Magic came from a big city, Lansing, Michigan, and Larry from a small rural community. Magic was black, and Larry was white. It might have mattered to some people but not to the two players. In their first meeting, in the "Final Four," they respected each other's

Ever since he saw his brothers wipe the bottom of their basketball shoes, Larry Bird has done the same. He does this to improve the traction of his shoes.

basketball ability. After both had become stars in the NBA, their natural rivalry grew into warm admiration for each other. Magic has visited Larry in French Lick. They have many things in common beyond great basketball ability. Larry is one of six children, and Magic has nine sisters and brothers. Larry's parents both worked hard. Magic's dad held two jobs to keep his family together. Larry Bird and Magic Johnson are very much alike. Both hold family values in high esteem. Each had considered the other the best player in the NBA. They have both been voted Most Valuable Player in the NBA three times. Bird or Johnson was the MVP six times in seven seasons, 1984 through 1990.

A closely guarded Larry Bird. Opponents fear his deadly three-point shot.

Magic Johnson and Michigan State ended Indiana State's unbeaten streak, 75–64. They double-teamed Larry Bird and held him to 19 points. He had averaged 28.6 during the season. However, Larry was named the College Basketball Player of the Year for 1978–79. He was headed for the NBA and so was Magic Johnson. Larry Bird went back to Terre Haute, where Indiana State is located, and graduated in June. He was eager to start his professional basketball career.

Larry Bird left for Boston armed with good advice. Four leading businessmen in Terre Haute had formed "The Committee." They helped Larry find the best agent to handle his contract with the Celtics. Bob Woolf, an attorney who represented many top stars, was the one Larry picked. When Larry moved to Boston, he bought a house next door to Bob Woolf's house. Larry and his girlfriend, Dinah Mattingly, became close friends of Bob and Annie Woolf and their children. Larry has always been lucky to have wise and experienced people around him, and he has been smart enough to listen to them. The millions of dollars he has earned have been wisely invested. He has been free to concentrate on being the greatest basketball player he can be.

Larry checked in at the Celtics' rookie camp and began his career in pro basketball. The fans and the press had already welcomed him. They expected that he would lead the Celtics back to the top of the NBA. It was different when Larry met his new teammates. They would make him prove how good he was.

The player who tested Larry the hardest was Cedric Maxwell. He was the key player on the Celtics and proud of it. He wanted Larry Bird to make good. Everyone would play better if Larry lived up to expectations. That is the way it worked out. When the Celtics won their next NBA title, Cedric Maxwell was the MVP in the playoffs.

Larry also had to show his new coach, Bill Fitch, that he would learn to play "the Celtics' way." It did not take long. As always, Larry was the first to arrive for practice and the last to leave. He passed the ball to any teammate who had a better shot. He hurried back down the court quickly on defense. It was clear that Larry Bird had great talent. What the coach and the other players also liked was his great attitude. He was a "team player."

Larry Bird's first test as a professional came in an exhibition game. The Boston Celtics and the Philadelphia 76ers were traditional rivals. The Sixers were heavily favored when the teams met in Madison Square Garden in New York City. Larry would play against the most exciting player in basketball. Julius Erving had led the way to a new style of playing. It depended on speed and great leaping ability. Erving, who was called Dr. J., seemed to hang in the air when he went up for a shot. Bird came from the traditional style of play. The idea was to be patient. You moved the ball around until someone got open. A well-placed shot by Larry Bird swishes through the strings of the net. Players like Dr. J. score their points with a slam dunk that rattles the backboard.

The preseason game would not count in the standings. However, Madison Square Garden was jammed with fans. Reporters from everywhere covered the game. It was the start of the "Bird Era." People wanted to know if the Celtics would once again become NBA champions. Larry's job was to guard Julius Erving. He did it well, although the Sixers beat the Celtics easily, 115–90. However, Larry Bird had passed his first test. The reporters crowded the dressing rooms of both teams after the game. They wanted to know what Julius Erving thought of the new kid on the block. Dr. J. told them, "He can play. He moves real good. You can feel his intensity. I am very favorably impressed with him as a player."

Larry puts everything he has into basketball. Constant practice has always been his trademark.

Larry said he was glad it was over. "When the game started, all I could think of was stopping Julius Erving. I wasn't thinking about my offense at all." Erving had missed his first three shots, and Larry played the rest of the game with great confidence.

The Boston Celtics opened the 1979–80 season at home. The Boston Garden was packed with fans. They hoped that Larry Bird would prove how good he was. The Houston Rockets were a real test. They were led by Moses Malone, last year's MVP. He was a center and dominated the action under the backboards.

The Celtics lived up to the hopes of their fans. They not only won, 114–106, but they also played as a team. Some

Larry Bird's agressive style of play got him into foul trouble in his first regular season professional game.

were veterans of past seasons, and others had come in trades. Larry Bird was the only rookie in the lineup. In the season's opener, Larry's aggressive play got him into foul trouble. He played only 28 minutes. He scored a respectable 14 points. He also grabbed 10 rebounds and had 5 assists to do his share in winning the game.

It did not take long for the Celtics to show they were back on track. They won 15 of their first 20 games. They played with the tight-knit teamwork of past Celtic teams. It was clear that Larry Bird made the difference. Just as Cedric Maxwell had hoped, Bird made his teammates better players. It had been the same in high school and college. While Larry Bird lacks the speed and jumping ability of most NBA forwards, he makes up for these shortcomings by anticipation. He has exceptional vision. He seems to know where everyone is on the court. He senses what they are about to do. Larry Bird acts on this instinct smartly. His passes lead teammates who then score on easy lay-ups. He steps into the other team's passing lanes and steals the ball. As Red Auerbach explained after Larry won the Rookie of the Year honors, " Larry never was really a rookie. He played like a veteran from the start."

Chapter 4

The Boston Celtics began a new dynasty for the 1980s—the "Bird Era." Boston was back in the playoffs at the end of Larry Bird's first season. The next season Larry would lead the Celtics all the way to the NBA championship. After that the question became, "Could they win NBA titles back-to-back?" It had not been done since the pre-Bird Celtics did it in 1968 and 1969.

The team added Danny Ainge to the backcourt. He had passed up professional basketball to play big league baseball with the Toronto Blue Jays. Now he had decided to switch back to basketball, and the Celtics had him. Young Danny Ainge would take the pressure off the Celtics' older guards. He was a deadly three-point shooter and an exciting ball handler. Like Larry Bird, he could use either hand equally well. They both wrote and ate lefthanded, but controlled the ball with the right hand. Players who are ambidextrous can pass or score by using either hand when necessary.

Although they were the defending champs and seemed even stronger, the Celtics started slowly. Then Larry Bird got

Danny Ainge joined the Celtics in 1981. Like Bird he could pass and score with either hand.

hot. He had two triple doubles in three nights. This is the term used when a player has double figures for points, assists, and rebounds. The Celtics ran up a new team winning streak. They won 18 in a row. Then Larry took a vicious elbow in the face. He lay without moving for a long time before being helped to the locker room. Larry got back into the game and even slam-dunked the winning points to beat the league-leading Milwaukee Bucks, 106–102. Then X-rays taken after the game showed he had a fractured cheekbone. Larry could not play. When he did come back, he played as "the sixth man." He played less time than usual but substituted in key situations. Only a dedicated team player could do such a thing. It resulted in a Celtics' season record of 63–19.

Larry's own stats had improved over the previous season. He was named to the all-NBA first team. On January 31 he had won the MVP award in the All-Star game. An NBA playoff title would have capped a great season, but it was not to be. In the second round the Celtics met their usual rival, the Philadelphia 76ers. The series went the full seven games, but when the Celtics' playmaker, Tiny Archibald, was hurt in the third game, Boston went flat. Larry could not will the team to win. He had never completely regained his best form after his own injury.

After a typical summer back in Indiana, where his injuries healed, Larry Bird was ready for the 1982–83 season. Again the team seemed better. Quinn Buckner, another Indiana native who had starred at Indiana University, joined the team. However, the Sixers gained from Houston Moses Malone, last year's MVP. He was to win his third MVP with Philadelphia for the coming season.

Larry got off to the greatest start of his career and carried the Celtics with him. Yet, when their record stood at 18–4, they were tied with Philadelphia. The Los Angeles Lakers in

Though the 1980s have been called the "Bird Era," the Celtics are a closely-knit team where everyone contributes to getting the ball to the man with the best chance of scoring.

the other division were also 18–4. It was to be that kind of season. The two top teams in the East were matching each other, and whichever won could expect to take on the Lakers for the NBA championship.

Professional athletes rarely risk "calling the shot." Babe Ruth did it once in a World Series. He said he would hit a home run and did it. Larry did something of the sort at Phoenix on February 26. He was playing on a badly sprained ankle. There was one second left in a game the Celtics were losing 101–100. The Phoenix Suns counted their chickens too soon. One player taunted Larry that they would stop him on the last play of the game. Larry answered back by saying he would personally score the winning basket. The ball was in-bounded to Bird, who took it with his back to the basket far beyond the three-point line. He whirled and shot. Swish. Larry ran off the court laughing.

On March 30 Larry set a new Celtic single-game scoring record of 53 points. The Celtics were playing winning basketball, but the Sixers, with Moses Malone, were five games ahead of them. Boston began to let down and ended with a 56–26 record. It was the first time they had won less than 60 games since the "Bird Era" began.

The Celtics played badly in the playoffs. They did not have to worry about Philadelphia. The Milwaukee Bucks knocked the Celtics out of the playoffs in the first round in four straight. The blame was placed on coach Bill Fitch. The team's morale was very low. Except for Larry Bird, who thrived on hard work, the others objected to the way Fitch drove the team. Everyone was relieved when K. C. Jones was made coach for the coming season. He had been an assistant coach and had been a great Celtic player. Larry Bird went home determined to improve his game even more. He practiced on the court beside his mother's house. He ran three or four miles a day. He thought hard about what could be done to help the Celtics return to the top of the NBA.

Once again the smart general manager, Red Auerbach, had swung a deal to improve the Celtics. The 1983–84 team would have Dennis Johnson. He had been named to the NBA's All-Defensive team the past five seasons, playing with Phoenix and Seattle. He mixed very well with the Celtics' veterans, particularly with Larry Bird.

One thing the Celtics had lacked at the end of the last season was a fighting spirit. Larry set out to show the rest of the league how tough Boston was. The exhibition season opened in the Boston Garden against their old enemy, the Philadelphia 76ers. Last year, after the Celtics had been eliminated, the Sixers had won the championship. On top of that, Moses Malone was voted the league's MVP again. The Sixers set out to physically intimidate the Celtics right there on their home court. The game had just begun when Moses Malone tackled Cedric Maxwell. Max threw the ball at him. Less than a minute later Larry cut himself in on the action. He and Mark Iavaroni grabbed each other's shirt. Larry hit the big man in the mouth and went after the even bigger Malone. Most brawls between athletes are just pushing and shoving matches. The players have never learned how to fight. Larry came from the hardscrabble country of southern Indiana. Boys grew up fighting to hang on to the few things they owned. Larry was a devastating battler.

Before the melee was over, Red Auerbach had his glasses off and was in Malone's face out on the floor. Red and Larry drew big fines from the NBA, but they had made their point. No one was going to push the Celtics around this season. The Boston Celtics romped through the schedule. By the end of January they had won 35 and lost only 9 games. They ended with 62 victories—the best record in the league. They

Dennis Johnson, a new Celtics member for the 1983-84 season, gets a hug from teammate Kevin McHale after a victory.

expected to meet the Sixers in the final round of the Eastern Conference playoff. Instead, Philadelphia was knocked off by the New Jersey Nets. The Celtics' toughest challenge came from the New York Knicks.

Bernard King was the fabulous star of the Knicks. It seemed certain that either he or Larry would be voted MVP for the season. The momentum in the playoff series swung back and forth. Finally it came to a seventh game at Boston. The series had been furiously fought. There had been ten technical fouls called. There were three ejections and one bench-clearing brawl. Larry Bird finally settled things by

Red Auerbach legendary general manager of the Boston Celtics with his trademark cigar, holds one of many Celtics trophies.

simply playing the finest playoff game of his career. He had 28 points at the end of the first half. That was more than Bernard King would score in the whole game. He ended the third quarter with a three-pointer. Bird outplayed King in every phase of the game. He averaged 30.4 points, 10.6 rebounds, and 7.1 assists. He shot 58.5 percent and sank 90 percent of his foul shots.

The Celtics were out to avenge their four straight losses to Milwaukee in last year's playoffs. The Celtics wiped out the Bucks in five games. They were back in the final round of the NBA playoffs for the first time in three years.

It would be Larry Bird against Magic Johnson once more. That's the way the public looked at it. Both players saw it differently. Magic and Larry played different positions. The Celtics counted on Larry Bird to score most of the team's points. Kareem Abdul-Jabbar, a seven-foot center, was the Lakers' scoring threat. Magic Johnson's role was passing and defense.

The Celtics were almost wiped out in four straight games. Only a bad play by the Lakers made a Celtic win possible in game two. In game four Larry Bird rallied his team, almost coming to blows with Kareem. With 16 seconds left to play, Larry tied the score. The game went to overtime. Then Larry made a game-winning 16-foot turnaround shot. The series was tied at two games each.

Game five, at the old Boston Garden, gave the Celtics a unique home-court advantage. The air conditioning broke down, and it was 97 degrees on the court. The Lakers could hardly breathe. It did not bother Larry. He hit on 15 of 20 shots and had 17 rebounds. He scored 34 points and outlasted everyone on the floor. The series went back to the West Coast. Once more the Lakers tied the series. Once again it would take a seventh game to decide the NBA title. Back in Boston, the

Celtics won their fifteenth NBA title. It was their second in the "Bird Era." Larry was the MVP in the playoffs and was also voted the MVP for the NBA season for the first time. He was at the peak of his career.

Before he went home for the summer, Larry did a very nice thing. The Celtics had an elderly equipment man. He had been with the team since the first NBA season, 1949–50. Larry told the Celtics he wanted to buy Walter Randall a championship ring. No one had every done anything like this. It made the last year of Walter's life happier. He died of cancer during the next season.

Larry Bird is not a player to rest on his laurels. He keeps improving because he can motivate himself year after year. Bird saw the coming 1984–85 season as another challenge. Gerald Henderson, the Celtics' high-scoring guard, had been traded. So, Bird's role would change. Instead of setting up baskets for others, he would take more shots himself. He would be the team's main scorer. He worked hard all summer to make this part of his game even better.

Chapter 5

The Celtics began the new season where they had left off. They won steadily. Larry was hot, and the Sixers were again the team to beat. Even with Moses Malone, Philadelphia's main man was still Julius Erving. He and Larry Bird were head-to-head rivals. The first meeting of the new season ended in a pushing match. Larry outscored Dr. J. 42 points to 6, and Erving did not like it. Both players were fined $7,500. People joked that the two rivals could pay with the money they made doing TV commercials together. They were friends off the court, but neither wanted to be second best when they played each other.

The Celtics seemed to be even better than the year before. They ran off long winning streaks. Games often ended with a spectacular shot by Larry Bird. Portland was about to beat the Celtics in the Boston Garden. Only one second remained, and the Trail Blazers led, 128–127. Larry took a downcourt pass in the left corner. With two players all over him, he shot as he fell out of bounds. The ball went high in the air. It passed over a corner of the backboard and fell through the net for another impossible victory.

Injuries are part of the long NBA season, and Cedric Maxwell blew out his knee. Kevin McHale became a starter to stay. He broke Larry's single-game scoring record of 53. McHale got 56 on March 3. Nine days later Larry reclaimed the record. He tossed in 60 points against the Atlanta Hawks. Then an injury caught up with Larry Bird. His elbow, banged hard so many times when he dove for loose balls, hurt badly. He could play, but it was painful to shoot.

The Celtics made quick work of Cleveland to open the 1984–85 playoffs. Next came the Detroit Pistons. Larry had several great games and some bad ones, but the Celtics won. He took off the protective elbow pad and got ready for the conference finals against the familiar rivals, the Philadelphia 76ers. The Celtics won in five games when Larry stole the ball with four seconds to play. It saved a 102–100 victory. However, the stat sheets showed that Larry was not scoring his usual numbers. Against Detroit his shooting average fell below his season average. Against Philadelphia he dropped even farther. His elbow still hurt, and he played the Sixers with a bandaged finger.

The Los Angeles Lakers were favored in the final round. Larry Bird was slowed down by a chronic bad back, plus his elbow and finger problems. As a result, the Celtics were the underdogs. Amazingly, they trounced the Lakers 148–114 in the opener. Then a Kareem elbow added a bloody nose to Larry's list of injuries. Still, the Celtics fought on. In game four, in danger of falling behind three games to one, Boston trailed 92–85 with less than 10 minutes to play. Larry's eight unanswered points put the Celtics in the lead temporarily. With 12 seconds left, the score was tied. The Lakers looked for Larry to take the final shot. He crossed them up. He spotted Dennis Johnson wide open. D.J. hit a 20-footer just ahead of the buzzer. That was it for the Celtics, however. Larry shot badly, the team lost the next two, and the Lakers wrapped up the title. Larry Bird took one trophy back to Indiana. He was voted MVP for the NBA a second straight time.

The 1985–86 season would be another great one for Bird and the Celtics. Red Auerbach had worked another of his surprise additions to the team. He traded Cedric Maxwell for the one-time superstar, center Bill Walton. He had been the MVP back in 1977–78 and had led the Portland Trail Blazers to the NBA championship the season before. Then he had to give up the game. He had fragile feet. Stress fractures would not heal. Walton had reconstructive surgery done. Now, after being out of the game for five years, the Celtics brought him back. They hoped he could give them 20 minutes a game—long enough to rest Robert Parish.

Larry Bird played far below his usual form when the season began. His chronic back problem slowed him down. Then he found a trainer who had helped other athletes get back into action. Dan Dyrek got Larry into shape to play again. He was back in form for the All-Star game. For the first time the game featured a three-point shooting match. The eight best players in the NBA at sinking long shots were invited. They would have 60 seconds to get off 25 shots. Larry loved it. It was like being back in an Indiana gym and being challenged by his friends. One winning strategy was to "psych out" the others. Larry asked them, "Since my name is already on the check, which of you is going to get second-place money?" He had another way to upset his competition. When the others took off their sweats, Larry kept his on. Larry's edge was his size. He was a lot bigger than the others. He was 6 feet, 9 inches, and they averaged 6 feet, 3-1/2 inches. They

Injuries have forced Larry Bird out of a number of games, but he always manages to bounce back. Trainer Dan Dyrek helped Larry get back into action during the 1985-86 season.

shot three-pointers as jump shots. The taller Bird simply lofted them on their way. As the others tired, Larry got better. He hit 18 of his 25 shots in the final round. The three-point play is a Larry Bird specialty. In one nine-game stretch he hit on 25 of 34. This is a 73.5 percent average. Many NBA players do not shoot that well from the foul line.

The Celtics romped to their best team record, 67–15. Bill Walton played like Red Auerbach had hoped he would. The team looked ahead to the NBA playoffs. The Celtics wanted revenge. The public wanted to see Larry Bird and Magic Johnson play against each other again. Could Walton handle Kareem Abdul-Jabbar? As has happened before in the NBA, the matchup the public expected never took place. Houston would be the Celtics' opponents for the league championship. Bill Fitch, the former Boston coach, was now in charge of Houston.

It was an up-and-down series. The Celtics won the first two games in Boston but played poorly in Houston. They managed to squeeze out a 106–103 victory in the fourth game. However, the Rockets won game five when another battle erupted. The Rockets' massive 7-foot, 4-inch Ralph Sampson threw an elbow at 6-foot, 1-inch Jerry Sichting. Like Larry Bird, Jerry was a hard-nosed player from the tough southern Indiana country. He challenged the towering Sampson. Both players were put out of the game. Even with the dominating Sampson banished, the Celtics floundered. It would take a trip back to Boston to end the series.

The Celtics were keyed up. They hammered the Rockets hard. "No one, except the Chicago Bears, has ever played a first quarter as aggressively as we did," said Coach K. C. Jones. The Celtics led by wide margins all through the game. They were ahead 55–38 at the half and won 114–97. Larry had a "triple-double": 29 points, 11 rebounds, 12 assists. He also had three first-half steals and was named MVP for the playoffs. A little later he learned he was voted MVP for the league for the third straight time. The Boston Celtics were again the champs. The dynasty could go on and on. However, Larry Bird had played in pain for a year and a half. What's more, the Celtics made a great pick in the 1986 college draft. They took Len Bias of Maryland. He had been at the Celtics' rookie free-agent camp the year before. There Red Auerbach had learned how talented he was. He was like a Michael Jordan, only bigger. Larry Bird was so happy with the choice that he said he would come to the rookie camp himself. He would report a month early just to help Bias break in.

Then tragedy struck. Two days after the draft, Len Bias died of a drug overdose. He was twenty-two years old and partying in his dorm. The news shocked the sports world. The gifted young man who would have eventually replaced Larry Bird was another victim of drugs. In his autobiography, *Drive,* Larry Bird wondered: "How many great athletes have to die or have their careers ruined before they get the message?"

It was a more mature Larry Bird who spoke his mind. He changed his summer activities. He still found time to share with old friends but also began new business ventures. He had known of other superstars whose fortunes had been lost in bad deals. He still had the advice of "The Committee" to guide him. He liked the idea of owning a four-floor hotel in Terre Haute. It is called, "Larry Bird's Boston Connection." There are three different restaurants in the hotel. Larry's trophies and awards are kept in one of them. There is a gift shop with a line of Larry Bird and Boston Celtics items. T-shirts, replica jerseys with number 33, posters, etc., are sold there.

Larry's hotel and three restaurants give jobs to local people. He also owns a car sales business in the small town of

Larry Bird hoists the 1986 NBA Championship trophy over his head at the Celtics celebration in Boston.

Martinsville, Indiana. People will drive hundreds of miles to have a Larry Bird sales decal on their car or pick-up truck.

The loss of Len Bias was felt by the Celtics during the 1986–87 season. Larry's lists of injuries grew. He hurt both Achilles tendons. He missed games and had to limit his practice time while they healed. The Celtics lacked good players on the bench. Bill Walton's foot problems returned, and he missed almost the whole season. Then Kevin McHale also broke his foot. He managed to play, but the team was struggling. Coach K. C. Jones had to keep his few quality players in the game too long. They wore out as the season went on. The specter of Len Bias would haunt Larry Bird's remaining years.

The Celtics were almost unbeatable at home. They won 39 games and lost only 2. On the road, however, they had a losing record. For the first time since the 1982–83 season, they did not lead the league in victories. The Lakers did. The Celtics managed to win the Eastern Division Conference championship. However, the Lakers, with Magic Johnson as the MVP of the playoffs, won the NBA championship in six games. Magic Johnson also ended Larry Bird's hold on the league's Most Valuable Player title. After three straight years, Larry was replaced by Magic.

The next year the Lakers continued to be the NBA's dominant team. They became the first team since the Celtics of 1968 and 1969 to win back-to-back titles. The Celtics did not even make the finals in 1988. The Detroit Pistons were now the Eastern Conference champions. Basketball fans wondered if the reign of Larry Bird and the Boston Celtics was over. Had the Celtics' new dynasty ended? Would Larry Bird lead them back to the top? He would turn thirty during the coming season. How long could he continue to throw his body into game after game?

Chapter 6

In the summer of 1988, Larry Bird's agent Bob Woolf, was negotiating a new contract with the Celtics. Boston had already reached the NBA cap on player salaries, so they wouldn't be able to offer Larry more money then he was already making. Instead, his new contract called for a salary of $2.2 million and a nearly $5 million bonus just for signing the contract. It was agreed that Larry would put off receiving the bonus until 1991.

This signing bonus would cause some controversy in the summer of 1991 when the New York Knicks' Patrick Ewing tried to renegotiate his contract. The bonus added to Larry Bird's salary for the 1990–91 season would total $7.1 million, making him the highest paid player in the league, pushing Ewing to the Number Five spot. Ewing's contract said that if he were not among the four highest paid players in the NBA, then he would be able to renegotiate his contract. In the end, a mediator decided that Larry's signing bonus did not count as salary. Therefore, Ewing was the fourth highest paid player in the league and was unable to renegotiate.

Bird was almost totally inactive during the 1988–89 season. His total season record amounted to eight preseason and six regular season games. Larry had been having some ankle trouble for the past few seasons. He would occasionally pull or strain his Achilles tendons. Stretching seemed to relax the muscles, but warm-up sessions were taking much longer. Eventually this condition developed to the point where his ankle muscles would not stay loose and began to swell.

A CAT scan revealed that a spur (a bony growth) in Bird's right ankle had grown enormously. Larry's doctor decided to remove the spur surgically and predicted that Larry would be able to return to the court in March 1989. After surgery, Larry went through a strict routine of therapy, exercise, and stretching. He did whatever he could to get back into the lineup. He attempted to return in March, but his foot was still not completely healed. He stayed out for the rest of the season.

Boston wound up with only 42 wins that season and finished in third place in the Atlantic Division of the Eastern Conference. They were blasted out of the quarterfinals three games to none by the Detroit Pistons. Detroit went on to win their first ever NBA championship, sweeping the defending champion Los Angeles Lakers in four straight games.

Larry returned for the 1989–90 season eager to give the Celtics another winning season. But it was a new team from the one he left in 1988. K. C. Jones had been replaced by Jimmy Rodgers as the new Celtics coach. Danny Ainge had been traded to Sacramento. Brian Shaw left the Celtics to play in Italy. Tough, talented, and effective on the court, the older core of Bird, Parish, and McHale needed younger skilled players to back them up. But the backup players just were not there, and the regulars had to play longer in each game. As a result, Boston was wearing out its best players.

Larry Bird with teammate Reggie Lewis.

A high point for Larry in the season was his sinking of 71 consecutive free throws, coming close to the record of 78 set by Calvin Murphy. The Celtics finished in second place in the Atlantic Division, with 52 wins and 30 losses. On May 6, the Knicks knocked out Boston in the first round of playoffs three games to two.

At the end of the 1989–90 season, Chris Ford replaced Jimmy Rogers as Boston's coach. Ford had been an assistant Celtics' coach for seven years. Under Coach Ford, the 1990–91 season began well for Bird and the Celtics. The team had made a number of changes in their style of play, including minimizing the use of the three-point shot. The Celtics were known for using the three-point shot to help them win games and had led the league in the number of three-pointers taken. With the decline in the use of this tactic, Larry Bird could no longer call himself "the three-point king." Bird's position also changed. He was now power forward. But his chronic back problems forced him out of the lineup—indefinitely. Following this injury, it was rumored that he might announce his retirement at the end of the season.

In spite of Bird's injury, the Celtics won the Atlantic Division title with 56 wins and made it into the postseason playoffs. Larry had missed 22 games that season, but his fans were hoping that he would come back to play the Indiana Pacers in the Eastern Conference first-round playoffs.

Despite his sore back, Larry did come back and deliver a solid performance. Both Boston and Indiana played well and split the first four games. In the fifth and final game of the series, Larry hit his head on the floor as he dove for the ball. He made his way to the locker room, where the team doctor applied ice and did what he could for the bruise. In spite of the pain in his face combined with his back injury, Larry

Despite extremely painful injuries, Larry came back to help his team defeat Indiana in the semifinals of the Eastern Conference playoffs.

performed incredibly. The Celtics took the final game 124–121.

The Celtics now had to face the Detroit Pistons, two-time defending NBA champions, in the semifinals of the Eastern Conference. Larry sat out the first game due to his bad back, but came back in the second game. In the third game of the series, Boston handed Detroit a stunning defeat 115–83, the Pistons worst home game in three years. Larry played 33 minutes in the third game. He put in only 10 points, but offset that with 7 rebounds and 4 assists. The Celtics now had a two to one lead in the series, but their luck soon ran out. The next three games went to Detroit, and the Celtics were out of the playoffs.

Larry Bird stretches out in front of the Celtics bench during a game. His chronic back problem was finally treated in spring of 1991.

Larry Bird and the Celtics have a loyal following in Boston.

On June 8, 1991, Larry Bird walked out of New England Baptist Hospital. He had been there for surgery to relieve the back problems that had kept him out of 22 games the previous season. A bone fragment was removed from one of Larry's vertebrae. The fragment had put pressure on the nerve endings in the vertebrae, causing the pain in Larry's back. With no fragment, there was no pressure and therefore no pain. Dr. Arnold Scheller, the Celtics' team physician, said Larry's rehabilitation would include wearing a back brace and walking nearly ten miles each day.

Plagued by injuries in recent years, Larry Bird's time as the star of the Boston Celtics may be winding down. If his injuries become so severe he cannot play, Bird will be forced to retire. But Bird has always been a fighter, and his determination to win and excel may extend his career.

For now, it looks as though Larry Bird will continue to be a part of the Celtics' lineup. Boston is where Larry began as Rookie of the Year and where he became the NBA all-time three-point field goal leader. Bird went on to win three NBA Most Valuable Player awards and lead the Celtics to three NBA championships. He is a legend in basketball and in Boston, where he has joined the ranks of the Celtics' greats, Bill Russell and Bob Cousy. Boston loves the Celtics, and Larry Bird loves Boston. As Larry himself wrote, "I'll always be a Celtic."

In 1991, it was announced that Larry would become a part of the 1992 United States Olympic basketball team. This would be the first Olympic basketball team from the United States to feature professional athletes. Bird would be one of many greats on the team that would also include Magic Johnson, Michael Jordan, and Charles Barkley. After more than ten years in professional basketball, Larry Bird is still among the best in the NBA.

CAREER STATISTICS

COLLEGE

Year	Team	GP	FG%	REB	PTS	AVG
1976-77	Indiana State	28	.544	373	918	32.8
1977-78	Indiana State	32	.524	369	959	30.0
1978-79	Indiana State	34	.532	505	973	28.6
	TOTAL	94	.533	1247	2850	30.3

NBA

Year	Team	GP	FG%	REB	AST	STL	BLK	PTS	AVG
1979-80	Boston	82	.474	852	370	143	53	1745	21.3
1980-81	Boston	82	.478	895	451	161	63	1741	21.2
1981-82	Boston	77	.503	837	447	143	66	1761	22.9
1982-83	Boston	79	.504	870	458	148	71	1867	23.6
1983-84	Boston	79	.492	796	520	144	69	1908	24.2
1984-85	Boston	80	.522	842	531	129	98	2295	28.7
1985-86	Boston	82	.496	805	557	166	51	2115	25.8
1986-87	Boston	74	.525	682	566	135	70	2076	28.1
1987-88	Boston	76	.527	703	467	125	57	2275	29.9
1988-89	Boston	6	.471	37	29	6	5	116	19.3
1989-90	Boston	75	.473	712	562	106	61	1820	24.3
1990-91	Boston	60	.454	509	431	108	58	1164	19.4
	TOTAL	852	.497	8540	5389	1514	722	20883	24.5

Index

S

Sampson, Ralph, 46
Scheller, Dr. Arnold, 57
Seattle SuperSonics, 37
Shaw, Brian, 51
Sichting, Jerry, 46
Spectrum, 9
Springs Valley High School, 14,
        18, 20–21, 24

T

Terre Haute, Indiana, 27, 47
Three-point shooting match, 44,
        46
Triple-double, 46

U

United States Olympic
        basketball team (1992),
        57

W

Walton, Bill, 44, 46, 49
Woolf, Annie, 27
Woolf, Bob, 27, 50
World War II, 17

About the Author

Jack Kavanagh has shared with his children and grandchildren a lifelong love of sports and admiration for the players who bring values other than statistics and titles to their games. Putting it all into words in books such as this has been Mr. Kavanagh's own contribution to this link between generations.

CHILDREN'S ROOM

J
BIRD
KAV

Kavanagh, Jack.

Sports great Larry
Bird.

514508

DATE			